Space

A CHAPTER BOOK

BY ROSANNA HANSEN

children's press®

A Division of Scholastic Inc.

New York   Toronto   London   Auckland   Sydney
Mexico City   New Delhi   Hong Kong
Danbury, Connecticut

For Vicky and Jack, stars of the first magnitude

ACKNOWLEDGMENTS

The author would like to thank astronomer Roy Gallant, who first inspired her
interest in stars, planets, and space exploration. She would also like to thank the
astronomers, astronauts, and engineers at NASA and elsewhere whose expertise and
courage has enabled us to learn more about the mysteries of the universe.
In particular, warm thanks go to Dr. Jeffrey Kenney of Yale University for his helpful
comments on this book. In addition, the author would like to thank her terrific
publishing team: Catherine Nichols, Atif Toor, Laura Miller, Linda Falken, and
Nancy Hall. Their hard work and sound advice is much appreciated.

Library of Congress Cataloging-in-Publication Data

Hansen, Rosanna.
  Space : a chapter book / by Rosanna Hansen.
    p. cm. – (True tales)
Summary: Introduces the activities of humans in space, including the
Apollo 11 mission to the moon, Shannon Lucid's work on the Russian space
station Mir, the Hubble Space Telescope, and the Voyager missions to
Jupiter and Saturn.
Includes bibliographical references and index.
  ISBN 0-516-22919-2 (lib. bdg.)   0-516-24608-9 (pbk.)
  1. Astronautics–Juvenile literature. [1. Astronautics. 2. Outer
space–Exploration.] I. Title. II. Series.
  TL793.H3526 2003
  629.4–dc21
                          2003003915

CONTENTS

INTRODUCTION

What is our Moon made of? Can people live in **space**? How far away are the stars? For thousands of years, people have looked up at the night sky and wondered about the mysteries of space.

Today, we have learned the answers to these questions. Scientists (SYE-uhn-tiss) and **astronauts** have worked hard to find the answers for us. Some of them have even flown into space to learn about its mysteries.

Here are true stories of four amazing adventures in space, and the people who made them possible. Thanks to them, the **Universe** is no longer such a strange and mysterious place.

CHAPTER ONE

MISSION TO THE MOON

"Ten, nine, eight, seven, six, five…"

The three men listened, strapped into the ***Apollo 11* spacecraft**. In a few seconds, their huge rocket would blast into space. Astronauts Neil Armstrong, Edwin "Buzz" Aldrin, and Michael Collins had been on other space flights. *Apollo 11* was special. This time, they were going to the Moon!

Left to right: Neil Armstrong, Michael Collins, Edwin Aldrin

On July 16, 1969, *Apollo 11* blasted into space.

"…four, three, two, one…we have liftoff!" With a mighty roar, the rocket rose into the air. The ground shook. Flames and smoke blasted from the rocket's tail.

Inside, the
astronauts were shoved back
in their seats by the rocket's changing speed.
They were pulled from side to side as the
rocket rattled and shook. In minutes, the
rocket's first two parts fell away.

Apollo 11 was already more than a
hundred miles above Earth. Soon the men
started *Apollo's* engines again. Whoosh!
Apollo speeded up to 24,300 miles (39,196
kilometers) per hour. Now they were going
fast enough to escape Earth's gravity. Next
stop, the Moon!

Without the pull of **gravity** (GRAV-uh-
tee), the astronauts were **weightless**. They
could float around the cabin. Everything
floated, unless it was tied down.

For days, the astronauts traveled on and on through space. By the fifth day, *Apollo* was very close to the Moon. Now the astronauts needed to split the spacecraft in two parts.

Neil and Buzz would head for the Moon in one part. This part was named the *Eagle*. Michael would stay in the main part of the spacecraft. This part was called *Columbia*.

Neil and Buzz put on their spacesuits. Then they crawled into the *Eagle*.

Michael remained in *Columbia*. This picture was taken from the *Eagle*.

The *Eagle*

Slowly, the *Eagle* moved down toward the Moon. Suddenly, Neil saw huge stones in the *Eagle's* path. He quickly steered away from the stones. Next, he needed a new place to land. They were almost out of fuel.

At last, Neil saw a flat place. He set the *Eagle* down. "The *Eagle* has landed," he told **Mission Control**.

Neil and Buzz got ready to go outside. Then Neil opened the door. There was the moon, a silent, empty world.

Neil climbed down the ladder. As he climbed, 600 million people on Earth watched and listened. Then Neil stepped down on the Moon. He had done it! "That's one small step for a man, one giant leap for mankind," Neil said.

Neil walked a few steps. Then, he picked up some Moon rocks and dust to bring back. Soon Buzz joined him. Together, the

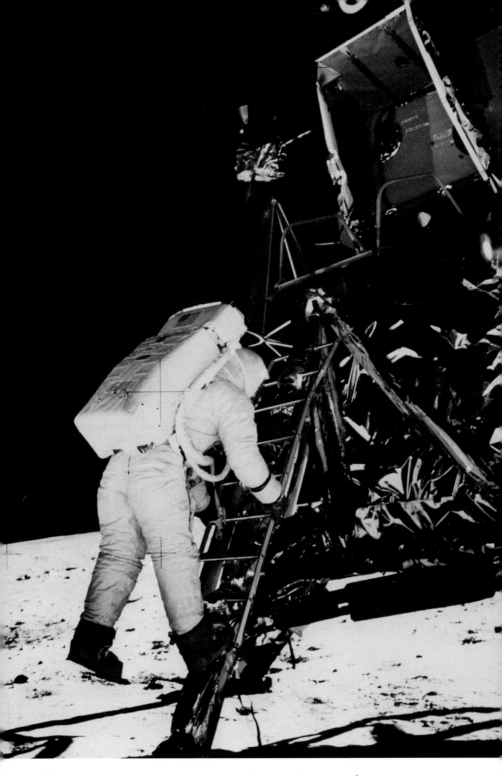

Buzz stepping down from the *Eagle*

An astronaut's foot and footprint

men walked into the strange, gray world of the Moon.

The men took big steps they called "kangaroo hops." The Moon has six times less gravity than Earth, so it was easy for the men to move.

It was time to get to work. The men planted an American flag and gathered more rocks and dust. They set up experiments to learn more about the Moon. They also took photos.

The surface of the Moon

An American flag on the Moon

Soon they needed to leave. Michael was waiting for them in the *Columbia*. Neil and Buzz got ready and started the *Eagle's* engine. After a few hours, the *Eagle* reached the *Columbia* safely. Soon, the men were ready to head back to Earth.

After three days, their spacecraft zoomed into view on Earth. A few minutes later, *Apollo 11* splashed down in the Pacific Ocean. The men were home!

These brave astronauts had completed the greatest space adventure of our time. Because of them, the Moon is not a strange and distant mystery.

A parade in New York City welcomed the astronauts home.

Earth as seen from the Moon

CHAPTER TWO

LIVING AND WORKING IN SPACE

In March 1996, astronaut Shannon Lucid blasted into space aboard the **space shuttle** *Atlantis.* Shannon was headed for the Russian **space station** *Mir* (MEER). There, she would live and work with the Russian **crew**.

Soon, the shuttle reached *Mir.* Shannon was excited to see her new home. She met the Russian crew, Yuri Onufrienko and Yuri Usachev.

Mir space station

Then, Shannon unpacked. She hung her sleeping bag on one wall of her room. She stuck her computer to the other wall with special tape. The tape kept her things from floating away.

Shannon Lucid aboard *Mir*

Shannon and the two "Yuris"

Shannon ate all her meals with her Russian friends. They liked to talk together. They especially liked to tell stories about their own countries. Soon Shannon had nicknamed her friends "the two Yuris."

During her stay in *Mir*, Shannon felt weightless. She felt this way because *Mir* was circling, or **orbiting**, Earth. During *Mir's* orbit around Earth, the spacecraft was flying forward and falling at the same time. This orbiting motion made Shannon feel weightless. She could float, and so could everything else.

Shannon on a treadmill

Shannon exercised for about two hours every day on *Mir*. She needed to exercise to stay strong. While Shannon was in orbit, there was no gravity pulling on her body. So, her bones and muscles started to shrink during her stay. They didn't have to work as hard on *Mir* as they do on Earth.

Exercise helps to keep bones and muscles from shrinking. That's why astronauts need to exercise as much as possible.

During her **mission**, Shannon had many science experiments to do. She planted

Shannon looks at wheat growing in a greenhouse.

During her stay on *Mir*, Shannon could sit without using a chair.

wheat seeds in a greenhouse. She watched baby birds grow, too.

Shannon also studied how living in a space station changes bones, muscles, and lungs. Her research is helping scientists plan longer space flights.

After six months, Shannon was ready to go home, but bad weather kept the shuttle grounded. Finally, *Atlantis* arrived to bring her home.

Atlantis space shuttle

Shannon floating through the tunnel from *Mir* to *Atlantis*.

When she landed back on Earth, Shannon had made history. She had set a new world record for the longest space flight by a woman. Her flight totaled 75.2 million miles in 188 days, four hours, and fourteen seconds. That's the longest any woman astronaut has ever stayed in space!

Shannon Lucid is a true space **pioneer**. Like most pioneers, she likes to think about new adventures. Her next dream is a trip to Mars. As Shannon once said, "I would really hope to see the day when we would be able to make a flight to Mars. And I'd love to be on it."

Mir **space station circling Earth**

CHAPTER THREE

TRAVELING TO THE STARS

In the summer of 1977, two spacecraft named *Voyager 1* and *2* blasted off from Earth. Today, more than twenty-five years later, they are still sailing through space. They have traveled much farther than any other spacecraft.

During their trip, the *Voyagers* sent us photos of the **planets** Jupiter, Saturn, Uranus, and Neptune. Thanks to the *Voyagers*, we learned much more about these planets than people had known before.

Voyager 1 being launched

Voyager 2 during liftoff

Sun Mercury Venus Earth Mars Jupiter Saturn Uranus Neptune Pluto

Our Solar System

The *Voyagers'* first mission was to visit the planets Jupiter and Saturn. These planets are very far away from Earth. They are the fifth and sixth planets in our **Solar System**.

Scientists wanted to learn more about these planets but Jupiter and Saturn were too far away for astronauts to visit. So the scientists sent *Voyager 1* and *2* instead. *Voyager 1* and *2* did not have people on board. They send photos and messages back to Earth by radio.

The *Voyager* spacecraft are not very big. They are about the size of a small car. They are strong, and they are speedy. They can zip through space at 35,000 miles (56,327 kilometers) an hour.

The *Voyagers* needed to be speedy. Back in 1977, they had very long trips ahead of them. To reach Jupiter, they had to sail through space for a year and a half.

Jupiter is a giant planet made of gas. It is so big that 1,300 Earths could fit inside it. It is truly king of the planets in our Solar System.

Picture of Jupiter from *Voyager 1*

Both *Voyagers* flew by Jupiter in 1979. They sent back 33,000 photos of Jupiter and its moons. We learned many amazing things from these photos.

First, we learned that Jupiter has a strange ring around it. The ring is less than one mile (0.6 kilometer) thick. It stretches out for 36,000 miles (58,000 kilometers).

We learned about the Great Red Spot on Jupiter, too. This "spot" is a huge storm of gases. The Great Red Spot is as big as planet Earth! The *Voyager* photos clearly showed this strange "spot" on Jupiter.

Jupiter's Great Red Spot

Jupiter and four of its largest moons

We also learned new things about Jupiter's moons. One of its moons is named Io. The *Voyagers* found **volcanoes** on Io! These volcanoes were the first ever found outside Earth.

Io's volcanoes blow up or explode. When they explode, they splash Io with bright colors. Io is splashed with yellow, orange, red, and white. It looks like a pizza!

Io looking like a pizza

29

This picture was taken when *Voyager 2* was 21 million miles (33.9 million kilometers) from Saturn.

After visiting Jupiter, the *Voyagers* flew on toward Saturn. This trip took more than three years.

Saturn is the second largest planet. It is big enough for 800 Earths to fit inside. Like Jupiter, it is made of gas. It is famous for its beautiful rings.

For years, scientists thought that Saturn had three huge rings around it. The *Voyagers* proved this idea was wrong. Saturn doesn't have three rings. It has over 1,000 rings! The rings are made of ice, rock, and dust.

Saturn has over 1,000 rings.

Uranus

Next, the scientists decided to send *Voyager 2* on toward more planets. It would visit the strange, faraway worlds of Uranus and Neptune.

The scientists had a different plan for *Voyager 1*. They sent it zooming far away from the planets, spinning out toward the edge of our Solar System. It was headed for the stars!

Neptune

Meanwhile, *Voyager 2* was flying toward Uranus and Neptune. These planets are very, very far away. It took *Voyager 2* over four years to reach them.

Voyager 2 found out most of what we know about Uranus and Neptune. In many ways, these planets are almost twins. They are both giant planets made of gas. They are both icy cold.

The two *Voyager* spacecraft were built to be twins and are exactly alike. This photo shows how they both look.

After its visit to Neptune, *Voyager 2* left the planets behind. Like *Voyager 1*, it headed out to the edge of our Solar System, and on to the stars.

As you read this, the *Voyagers* are still sailing out to the distant stars. They are still sending their messages back to Earth, too. Each year, they fly deeper and deeper into the Universe. Someday, the *Voyagers* may even reach another world with living beings, on a planet far, far away.

Distant galaxies

CHAPTER FOUR

LOOKING INTO DEEP SPACE

The Hubble Space Telescope can look deep into space. It can show us **galaxies** over twelve billion years old! That is almost as old as our entire universe.

The Hubble shows us stars being born, stars dying, galaxies forming, and much more. In fact, scientists say that the Hubble may be the most important telescope ever made.

The Hubble Space Telescope

The Hubble is named for Edwin P. Hubble, an important astronomer.

In 1990, the Hubble rocketed into space. The space shuttle carried it high into the sky. Now the Hubble circles Earth about 370 miles above us.

The Hubble gives us a clear view into space. On Earth, the air around us blurs our view. There is no air in space, so the Hubble can see better there. Today, it can see more clearly and ten times farther than the best telescopes on Earth.

Scientists were excited when the Hubble flew into space in 1990. They couldn't wait

Astronauts trained for the repair of the Hubble. They practiced underwater to prepare themselves to work in space.

to see its first photos. Surprise! The first photos were bad. They looked fuzzy and strange. The scientists were worried. What was wrong with the Hubble? Soon, they found the problem. The main mirror in the Hubble was not made correctly.

What could be done? The scientists made a daring plan. They made special new mirrors for the Hubble. The new mirrors would act like giant eyeglasses. They would help the Hubble see clearly.

In 1993, seven astronauts made a repair call in space. They flew to the Hubble in the space shuttle. There, they fit the new mirrors on the Hubble. They also fixed other broken parts.

Was the Hubble really fixed? No one knew for sure. Scientists had to **adjust** the new mirrors from Earth with their computers. After several weeks, the Hubble sent back new photos. Good news! The photos were clear, not fuzzy at all. The scientists were pleased. At last, the Hubble was as good as new.

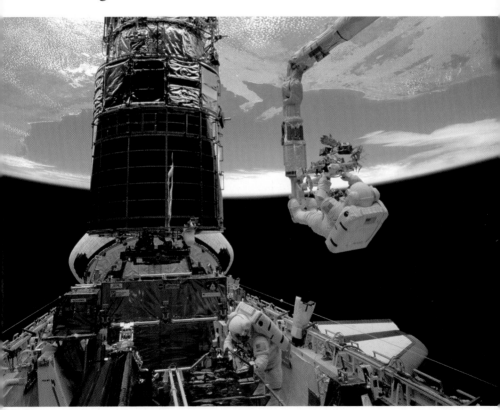

Astronauts repair the Hubble.

Photos taken by the Hubble Space Telescope

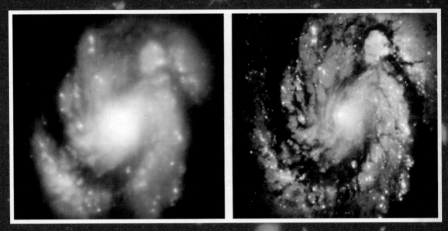

The Hubble's first photos looked unclear and fuzzy.
After it was fixed, its photos looked clear and sharp.

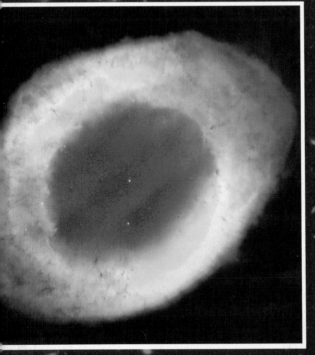

When stars die, they blow off their
outer layers of gases. This dying
star is in the Ring Nebula.

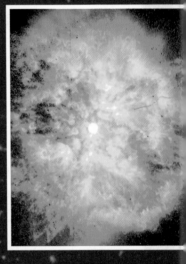

Blobs of gas from
a super-hot star
moving at speeds of
over 100,000 miles
(160,934 kilometers)
per hour

Two galaxies smashing into each other

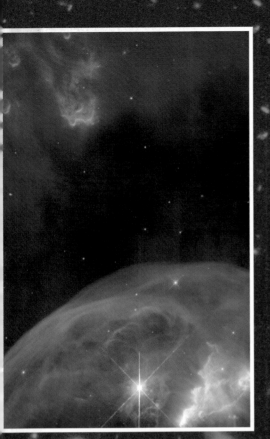

The center star in the Bubble Nebula is forty times larger than our Sun.

A tornado-like twister in the Lagoon Nebula

In the Eagle Nebula, shown here and on the cover, stars are born in a cloud of gas and dust.

One of the most beautiful photos taken by the Hubble is of the Eagle Nebula. A **nebula** is a giant cloud of gas and dust lit up by the stars that are forming inside it.

The Hubble is sending us more photos every year. If all goes well, it will continue to take photos until 2010. Then it will be brought back to Earth.

By 2010, a new space telescope may be in orbit. Scientists hope this new telescope will replace the Hubble.

As planned, the new telescope will look even deeper into space than the Hubble. It will help us learn how the first stars and galaxies were born. That will help us understand the very beginnings of our Universe.

A spiral galaxy

GLOSSARY

adjust to change or move something a little bit

Apollo 11 the spacecraft that brought humans to the Moon for the first time

astronaut a person who flies in a spacecraft

crew a group of people that work together

galaxy billions of stars which form a group

gravity (GRAV-uh-tee) the force that makes things move downward toward Earth

mission a special job to do in space

Mission Control the group of people on Earth who talk to and work with astronauts when the astronauts are in space

nebula a giant cloud of gas and dust lit up by the stars inside it

orbit to move in a circle around Earth or another heavenly body

pioneer a person who does something for the first time

planet one of the nine large bodies that circle our Sun

Solar System the Sun and all the planets and other objects that move around it

space the area in which the Universe exists

spacecraft a vehicle used to fly in space

space shuttle a spacecraft that takes people into space and brings them back again

space station a spacecraft that can circle Earth for a long time and where a crew can live for a long time

Universe everything there is

volcano a mountain with an opening through which fire, gas, and melted rock pour out

weightless free of Earth's gravity

FIND OUT MORE

Mission to the Moon
www.nasm.edu/apollo/AS11
Watch movies from the *Apollo 11* mission.

Living and Working in Space
http://spaceflight.nasa.gov/history/shuttle-mir/history/h-t-child-main.htm
Take a virtual tour of the space station *Mir*.

Traveling to the Stars
www.jpl.nasa.gov
The website has lots of information on *Voyager 1* and *2* and other space probes.

Looking into Deep Space
www.exploratorium.edu/hubble/index.html
See more photographs of deep space taken by the Hubble Space Telescope.

More Books to Read

Adventure in Space: The Flight to Fix the Hubble, by Elaine Scott and Margaret Miller, Hyperion, 1995

Destination: Space, by Seymour Simon, HarperCollins, 2002

First on the Moon: What It Was like when Man Landed on the Moon, by Barbara Hehner, Hyperion, 2000

Shannon Lucid, Space Ambassador, by Carmen Bredeson, Millbrook Press, 2000

Voyager, by Gregory Vogt, Millbrook Press, 1991

INDEX

PHOTO CREDITS

MEET THE AUTHOR

Rosanna Hansen has worked in children's publishing as a manager, editor, and author. Most recently, she served as publisher and editor in chief of Weekly Reader, supervising seventeen classroom magazines as well as books. Previously, she was group publisher of Reader's Digest Children's Books.

Hansen has written a number of children's books, including several on astronomy and space exploration. Her books on space include *Astronauts Today* and *Seeing Stars: The Milky Way and Its Constellations.* In addition, she has written two other books in the True Tales series (*Caring Animals* and *Animal Rescuers*). In her free time, she enjoys stargazing, volunteering with the Good Dog Foundation, and performing with music groups. She and her husband, Corwith, live in Tuckahoe, New York.